DK

LONDON, NEW YORK,
MELBOURNE, MUNICH, and DELHI

Senior designer Sonia Whillock-Moore
Senior editor Deborah Lock
Project designer Gemma Fletcher
Designers Hedi Hunter, Sadie Thomas, Pamela Shiels,
Mary Sandberg, Gabriela Rosecka, Lauren Rosier
Additional editing by Lorrie Mack, Elinor Greenwood
US editor Margaret Parrish
Photography Will Heap
Picture researcher Karen VanRoss
RHS consultant Simon Maughan

Category publisher Mary Ling
Production editor Clare McLean
Production controller Claire Pearson
Jacket copywriter Adam Powley

First published in the United States in 2010 by
DK Publishing
375 Hudson Street
New York, New York 10014

Copyright © 2010 Dorling Kindersley Limited
10 11 12 13 14 10 9 8 7 6 5 4 3 2 1
176268—12/09

All rights reserved under International and Pan-American
Copyright Conventions. No part of this publication may be
reproduced, stored in a retrieval system, or transmitted in
any form or by any means, electronic, mechanical, photocopying,
recording, or otherwise, without the prior written permission
of the copyright owner. Published in Great Britain by
Dorling Kindersley Limited.

A catalog record for this book is
available from the Library of Congress
ISBN 978-0-7566-5887-8
Color reproduction by MDP, UK
Printed and bound by
Toppan, China

Discover more at
www.dk.com

Contents

4-5 Ready and set

6-7 Help them grow!

8-9 **Top 10**: Tips for green gardening

10-11 Water, weed... and wait

12-13 Creative containers

1 hour 14-15 Dazzling decorations

3 days 16-17 Enchanted path

1 day 18-19 Garden buddy

Section 1: 20-21 Flowers and unusual plants

Top 10 22-23 Top 10: Quick-to-grow plants

7 weeks 24-25 Marigold fish

10 weeks 26-27 Flowerpot people

12 weeks 28-29 Poppy power

3 2530 60712 1819

1 day | 30-31 Fairy ring
12 weeks | 32-33 Floral tepee
Top 10 | 34-35 Top 10: Cool plants to grow
8 weeks | 36-37 Nasturtium nibbles
2 hours | 38-39 Window-box wildlife
1 hour | 40-41 Wild-West cacti
4 weeks | 42-43 Pets' corner

Section 2: 44-45 Vegetables, herbs, and fruits

6 days | 46-47 One-week sprouters
Top 10 | 48-49 Top 10: Sprouting seeds
4 weeks | 50-51 Windowsill watercress
4 weeks | 52-53 Radish racers
4 weeks | 54-55 Salad relay

Top 10 | 56-57 Top 10: Microgreens
9 weeks | 58-59 Crazy kohl rabi
4 weeks | 60-61 Taste of Asia
12 weeks | 62-63 Carrot companions
5 weeks | 64-65 Pizza garden
12 weeks | 66-67 Colorful kebabs
10 weeks | 68-69 Magic beans
1 day | 70-71 Herbal sun tea
12 weeks | 72-73 Strawberry boot
2 hours | 74-75 Red currant refreshments

76-77 The finish line

78-79 Glossary and Index

80 Acknowledgments

Find out more

The American Horticultural Society is one of the nation's oldest gardening societies. Its mission is to educate and inspire people to become successful, environmentally responsible gardeners. It's never too early to start. Check out the youth gardening section, and find out about local gardening organizations and activities. Now start digging!

For more information and to join, contact:
American Horticultural Society
7931 East Boulevard Drive
Alexandria, VA 22308
Tel. 1-800-777-7931
www.ahs.org

Ready and set

The key to having fun in the garden is choosing plants you not only like, but can also grow quickly and successfully. Here are a few things to think about when you're getting started and planning all the different things you want to cultivate.

How big is your space?

Plants come in all shapes and sizes, so even small spaces are useful. When you're making your choices, check to see how tall and wide each plant will grow so you know which plants suit your space.

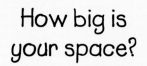

How much sunlight is there?

Different plants need different amounts of sunlight to grow, so check out how much light different parts of your gardening area get in a day. This information will be very useful for choosing suitable plants.

Symbol guide
What the lighting terms mean:

Full sun   Partial sun   Shade

For full sun, the plant needs 6 hours of direct sunlight each day. For partial sun, the plant needs 4-6 hours of direct sunlight each day. For shade, the plant needs very little direct sunlight, or none at all.

How much time do you have?

Some plants need lots of time and care, while others practically look after themselves. The projects in this book all feature plants that don't require much fuss.

Zucchinis will grow well with very little help from you, while tomatoes and fruit trees need a bit more attention.

Checklist

To make sure you're buying healthy plants from a garden center, check . . .

1 . . . that no pests are lurking on or under the leaves.

2 . . . that the leaves are not yellow or brown (which would indicate a stressed plant).

3 . . . that roots are not growing out of the bottom of the pot. (This means that the plant has been in the pot too long.)

4 . . . that the plant is short and stocky, not tall and thin (which would mean it hasn't had enough light).

5 . . . that the plant has no opened flowers. (Early flowering means the plant is stressed.)

Why not keep a diary?

Part of the fun of gardening (or any other sport or hobby) is seeing the results and learning what works and what doesn't. Try keeping a diary so you can record what you did and what you achieved.

Name of plant: Sunflower

Location (including the color or design of label or decoration used to mark the place): By the fence

Soil used: Potting soil

Date planted: April 12, 2010

If there's a seed packet or a plant label, paste it in.

3 weeks

10 weeks

Add photographs of progress labeled with the number of days and weeks old.

Include notes on care given: Water twice a week during the summer.

Help them grow!

Your job as a gardener will change as the plants in your garden grow, flower, fruit, and sometimes die back for the winter. Through its life, a plant needs to be cared for in different ways, from its early stages as a seedling to the time it fruits and makes seeds when it is grown.

START

1 Seed stage
A seed contains a new plant and a store of food to get it started. A gardener sows the seed at the correct planting depth and spacing.

2 Germination stage
A gardener provides warmth and moisture to help the seed get started. A propagator (see below) keeps the seed in a constant moist, humid condition.

3 Sprouting stage
A gardener makes sure the sprouting seed gets plenty of light so that it grows evenly and does not get too thin or spindly. Turn the pot every few days.

4 Seedling stage
A gardener makes sure the plant can make its own food by getting the right amount of sunlight and water. Protect the young plants from diseases and pests, such as slugs and snails.

Make a homemade propagator

You will need:
A large plastic bottle with lid
Scissors
A strip of cotton
A small plastic container

1 Ask an adult to help cut the plastic bottle in half using the scissors, and make a slit in the lid.

2 Insert a strip of cotton through the slit in the lid to act as a wick and screw the lid on the top bottle part.

Did you know?
An annual plant lives
for just one season,
while a perennial plant
grows back year
after year.

FINISH

5 Vegetative stage

A gardener makes sure the plant has enough water, light, soil, and food (fertilizer) so it can grow healthily. An unhealthy plant is more likely to get pests and diseases. Transfer the plant to a larger container if not directly sown outside.

6 Flowering stage

A gardener waters, puts in a plant stake to support a tall or climbing plant, and removes the dead flowers from an annual flower to lengthen the flowering period. Pinch out the growing tips of a flowering vegetable to encourage the plant to form large fruits.

7 Fruiting stage

A gardener can feed a plant with nutrients (fertilizer) to encourage fruiting. Seeds can be collected and sown again the following year, or left to fall on the ground, where they may germinate on their own. Some fruits are picked when ripe.

3 Add some water

into the base part, then put the top bottle part upside down into it, making sure the water level covers the lid and the cotton wick.

4 Fill the top

bottle part with soil. You are now ready to sow the seeds. (See page 66 for using this propagator for germinating zucchini seeds.)

5 After sowing

the seeds, cover with a small container that has holes punched in. Put the propagator in a warm and sunny place.

Tips for green gardening

In the world of gardening, there's an ever-increasing trend to use natural methods to keep plants healthy and control pests, to recycle garden waste, and to reuse everyday things. Why not give some of these top 10 tips a try?

1

A welcoming garden

Welcome friendly bugs that feed on insect pests. Ladybugs and lacewings eat aphids such as blackfly that destroy crops, so plant bright flowers such as candytuft, sunflowers, and marigolds and create places where these bugs can shelter and lay their eggs.

2

A bird-friendly garden

Welcome bug-eating birds, since they eat slugs, snails, grubs, caterpillars, and other pests that destroy plants. Put up birdfeeders and nesting boxes (including those you have made) to encourage more to visit.

We worms are fantastic compost makers. Garden waste and vegetable peelings are delicious for us to eat. After digesting, we leave casts (poop) that you can use as nutritious compost for your plants.

6

Homemade compost

Set up a compost bin in a warm, partly sunny site on top of some soil. A mix of vegetable peelings, garden waste, and fibrous woody brown material like paper or cardboard provide the right conditions for encouraging compost-making bugs. The rich, nutritious compost will be ready to use after six to nine months.

7

Use a wooden box with holes and a lid for a worm compost bin.

Worm composting

If you have only a little space, set up a home for some small, red tiger worms, which you can buy. Add a layer of moist, shredded newspaper and soil for their bedding, and then feed them once a week with vegetable peelings wrapped in newspaper or paper towels. Every two or three months, the rich, fine compost will be ready to use.

3

Companion planting
Companion planting, where two or more plants are grown close together, can sometimes help to ward off pests. Marigolds are believed to deter flying insect pests and soil pests from nearby crops. Grow a variety of plants to prevent one crop from being devastated by pests or disease.

4

Stop the slugs and snails
Slugs and snails can be formidable pests. Around containers, a band of copper, water-displacement spray, or petroleum jelly can deter them. Barriers such as grit and crushed eggshells scattered around plants can also be tried. Slug pellets that are not harmful to wildlife or children are the most reliable controls.

5

Traps for pests
Set up traps for garden pests, such as sticky yellow sheets to catch flying insects. To catch slugs, sink yogurt cups filled with milk or beer into the ground or leave some hollowed-out grapefruit halves around your plants.

8

Only make enough for what you'll need that day.

Compost and water

Cheese-cloth

Compost tea fertilizer
Although very smelly, compost tea is great as a natural fertilizer. Make your own by filling a small bucket a ¼ full of homemade compost and adding water to the top. Leave for three days, and then strain the mixture through cheesecloth into another bucket. Dilute the liquid with water before spraying.

9

Reuse plastic bottles
Plastic bottles can be reused in many ways around the garden. Cut off the bases and use them as warm, protective covers over seedlings or poke holes in their lids and use as a sprinkling watering device over seeds (see page 50). Turn to page 6 to find out how to use bottles to make homemade propagators.

10

Recycle packaging
Recycle all kinds of everyday packaging and old plastic and wooden containers as pots for plants. See page 12 for some creative ideas. Smaller containers can be used to get seeds started and then, once the seedlings become established, they can be transplanted into larger containers.

Water, weed... and wait

The secret of gardening is to look after your plants just like you would like to be looked after—like you, they get thirsty, they need protecting, and they don't like to be pushed around. For the quickest results, sow seeds directly into a container so they can be looked after more easily in a protected environment.

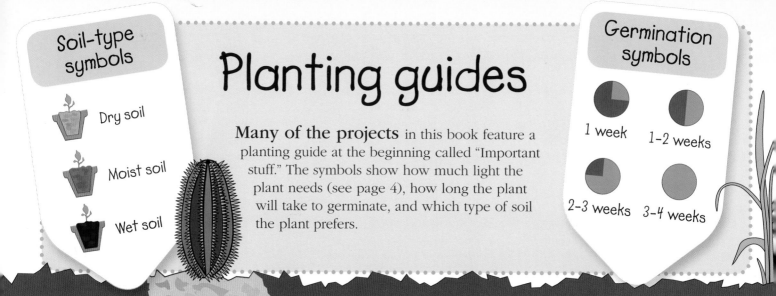

Soil-type symbols

Dry soil

Moist soil

Wet soil

Planting guides

Many of the projects in this book feature a planting guide at the beginning called "Important stuff." The symbols show how much light the plant needs (see page 4), how long the plant will take to germinate, and which type of soil the plant prefers.

Germination symbols

1 week

1-2 weeks

2-3 weeks

3-4 weeks

Make a self-irrigation system

You will need:

Plastic planter
Sheet of expanded polystyrene
Craft knife
Plastic pipe
Small plastic pot
(like a yogurt container)

1 **Ask an adult to cut a** polystyrene disk so it sits about 3 in (7 cm) from the base of your container. Make a hole in the center a bit smaller than your pot.

2 **Cut a length of** plastic piping a little longer than the height of the container, and make another hole in the edge of the polystyrene for this pipe.

Three top watering tips

1. Before sowing seeds, soak the soil and let the water drain through, then cover the seeds with dry soil, which is lighter than wet soil.

2. To ease a plant's stress when it's being transplanted, water it in its pot, water into the planting hole, and water it again after planting.

3. To make sure water reaches a plant's roots, half-bury next to it a plastic bottle with the top cut off and holes in its sides. Water into this.

Remember: In dry weather, plants get thirstier just like we do, so give them a big drink in the morning.

Mulching

Weeds compete for the same food and space as plants, and they often grow more quickly. To keep soil weed-free around your plants, use mulch—a thick layer on the surface of the soil that protects it and keeps moisture in (see below for suitable materials). Some mulch can attract helpful insects as well, or even improve the soil.

Small stones

Straw or fresh grass

Wood chips

Crushed egg shells

Turn to page 58 to see how this system was used to grow kohl rabi.

Put the container under cover if heavy rains are forecast. If you don't, it will become waterlogged.

3 **Punch holes** in the base of your small pot and tuck the pot underneath the hole in the polystyrene disk. Water will seep through the pot's holes from below.

4 **Place the pot** and polystyrene disk inside the container. Insert the pipe and fill the container (including the pot) with soil ready to sow some seeds.

5 **Pour water down** the pipe and into the reservoir underneath the polystyrene. It will seep up through the pot into the soil above and to the roots of your plants.

Creative containers

Unusual containers for your plants will make your gardening projects interesting. Any object that has sides can be used, so keep an eye out for possible ones to recycle and reuse.

Recycle food and drink containers.

Old boots or shoes

Use objects in a different way.

Wheelbarrow

Reuse old and broken objects.

Old watering cans

Top tip

When deciding what container would be best to use, think about the height and space the plants will need when they are fully grown.

Why not use old juice cartons?

12

Get ahead

If you can start early in the spring when the weather is still cold, get the seeds germinating indoors in these newspaper seed pots.

1 **Take a page** from a newspaper or comic strip. Fold over one long edge, twice. Roll the paper around a glass.

2 **Fold** the overlapping end of the tube inside the glass. This will become the base. Slide the paper off the glass.

3 **Looking** inside the tube, fold down the overlapping ends to make a base. Use the glass to flatten the base against a table.

4 **Fill the pot with soil** and then it is ready for sowing the seeds.

The newspaper pots will disintegrate when planted in the ground.

5 **Once the weather** is warmer outside, the seedlings can be planted in their newspaper pots directly into the soil, without disturbing the roots.

Get prepared

Whatever container you use, prepare it by following these steps:

1 **Ask an adult** to make some holes in the base to allow excess water to seep out. Use a liner with holes in if needed.

You could also use pieces of expanded polystyrene that small plants are bought in from garden centers.

2 **Put a layer** of gravel or broken pots in the base. This stops the soil from running out of the holes with the water.

3 **Fill the container** with suitable potting soil. Most plants are happy with all-purpose potting soil, but others have specific requirements.

Dazzling decorations

Colorful decorations poking up between your plants will not only add sparkle, but can also help to identify what you have planted, like a label. Make a note in your garden diary (see page 5) to say which design you've used for your gardening projects.

Flower

Bird

Butterfly

Did you know? Plants have two names: a scientific one often in Latin, and a common name, which may vary in different places.

You will need:

- Clean foil containers
- Scissors
- Black marker
- Colored markers
- Kebab sticks
- Glue
- Pen

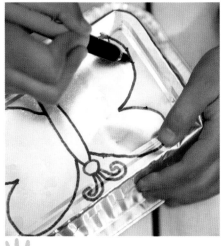

1 **Draw your design** onto the base of a foil container, using a black marker.

2 **Here are some ideas** for your design. You could choose bugs, flowers, and birds.

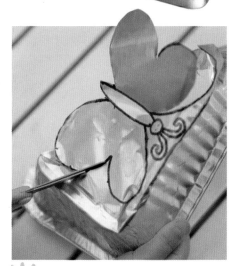

3 **Cut around the outline** of your design using a sharp pair of scissors.

4 **Press a pen** onto the foil shape to make raised holes.

5 **Color your design** with colored permanent markers and let the ink dry.

6 **Spread some glue** down the center of your design where the stick will go.

7 **Attach the stick** and hold it on the glue until it is secure.

8 **Turn to page 38** to see how this colorful butterfly looks great in a window box.

Enchanted path

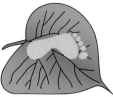

Dance along your very own winding path through your garden. Make these eye-catching stepping-stones by molding concrete into pretty leafy shapes. You'll need big leaves for this project, like the ones on rhubarb, zucchini, and sunflower plants.

You will need:

Disposable plastic gloves
Apron
Large plant leaves
Powdered cement mix
Large plastic container
Putty knife
Cardboard
Sand

1 **Mix up the cement** into a thick paste in a large plastic container, according to the instructions on the packaging. Remember to wear an apron and disposable plastic gloves.

2 **For each stone,** lay one leaf flat on a large piece of cardboard. The leaf's veiny reverse side should be facing up.

3 **With a putty knife,** spread the cement all over the leaf. This layer should be about ½ in (1 cm) thick at the edges, and at least 1½ in (4 cm) thick at the center.

4 **Smooth around** the edges and over the surface with your putty knife, then leave your concrete leaf for about two hours, until it's just dry enough to hold its shape.

5 **Gently turn it over and** peel away the leaf. This will be easier if the concrete is still a bit wet. Now leave the "stone" to dry completely for a day or two.

6 **Once your stones** are really dry, decide on their position by arranging them on the grass to make sure their spacing suits your stride.

7 **Use a trowel** to mark around each shape. Remove the first stone and dig out the grass and soil to the depth of the stone plus an extra 1 in (2.5 cm).

To level the stones, add or remove sand underneath.

8 **Place a 1 in (2.5 cm) layer** of sand into each hole and make sure it's smooth before placing the stone on top. Repeat for all your stones, checking that they're even and filling gaps around the edge with soil.

Top tip

Leave the stones to settle for a few days before walking on them.

Garden buddy

Plunder the recycling bin to create a wacky figure that will keep you company and help keep birds away from your plants. Form his body from cans and lids, then add detail using plastic, cardboard, or foil. When he's finished, hang him from a tree or tie him to a stake in the ground. Start by laying out your junk and planning where each piece will go.

You will need:

- Collection of junk
- Garden wire
- Wire from a coat hanger
- Scissors
- Glue

1 Gather all your cans. Ask an adult to make a hole in the base of each one by twisting in the point of one scissor blade until it punches through.

2 For the arms and legs, make a loop in one end of a length of garden wire and twist to secure. Thread the wire through one can, and leave the other end loose to connect to the body.

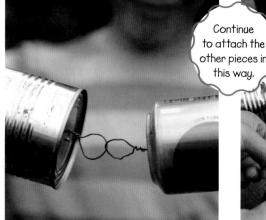

Continue to attach the other pieces in this way.

3 To attach the next can, loop a new piece of wire through the first loop before twisting to secure. Then thread this through the next can and make a loop at the other end.

4 For the body, make holes in opposite sides of a plastic bottle near the bottom. Insert a length of coat-hanger wire through them, looping to secure at each end. The legs will hang from this.

Do the same to attach the arms higher up the body.

5 For the figure's head, use a plastic flowerpot, then glue on bottle caps for the eyes and nose. A strip of foil will make nice shiny teeth.

CDs make shimmering reflections that will discourage hungry birds, so tuck a few of them inside your figure's body.

String for hair

Foil for hands

19

Ready set grow!

Flowers and unusual plants

Now that you're ready to begin, try out these fun projects. You can make a magical fairy ring and a window box for wildlife, create faces on sunflowers, and sculpt a Wild-West landscape. Your growing space can be transformed into a brightly colored, scented, and exciting area, all thanks to a few flowers and unusual plants.

12 weeks to go!

Start Poppy power on page 28

Start Floral tepee on page 32

9 weeks to go!

Tip: Cover the sunflower container with a clear polyethylene bag to keep the seeds warm while they germinate.

6 weeks to go!

Look for cacti and other succulents at a garden center.

3 weeks to go!

Look for ornamental grasses for the fairy ring in a garden center.

Countdown to flowering

11 weeks to go!

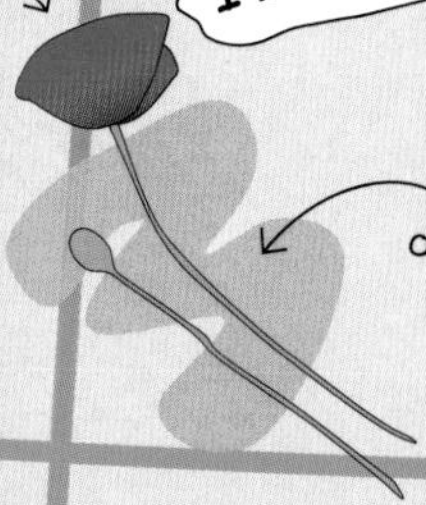

Thin seedlings to avoid overcrowding.

Seeds can be germinated indoors for an early start.

10 weeks to go!

Start Flowerpot people on page 26

8 weeks to go!

Start Nasturtium nibbles on page 36

7 weeks to go!

Start Marigold fish on page 24

5 weeks to go!

Tip: Water your plants regularly, especially during dry weather, and protect your young plants from slugs and snails (see page 9 for some advice).

4 weeks to go!

Start Pets' corner on page 42

2 weeks to go!

These projects only take a day to set up!

1 week to go!

Start Window-box wildlife on page 38
Start Wild-West cacti on page 40
Start Fairy ring on page 30

Quick-to-grow plants

All these plants grow quickly from seed so you don't have to wait long before something happens. When sowing directly, scatter the seeds and keep the soil moist so they germinate. Breaking off the dying flowers (deadheading) will lengthen the flowering period during the summer.

1

Love-in-a-mist *Nigella damascena*

Germinates in 2–3 weeks | 12 in (30 cm)

The fine hairlike bracts around the flowers give these plants their common name, "Love-in-a-mist." The flowers last for up to eight weeks in the summer and, if left, will then form balloonlike, striped seedpods.

2

Pot marigold *Calendula officinalis*

Germinates in 1–2 weeks | 5 in (12 cm)

These herb plants produce bright orange or yellow flowers. The spicy-tasting petals can be used in salads and savory dishes and for coloring cheese and butter. See page 24 for using marigolds to create a decorative floral fish shape.

3

Clarkia *Clarkia pulchella*

Germinates in 3 weeks | 16 in (40 cm)

Clarkia is named after the explorer Captain William Clark, who first saw this plant growing in the northwest of the United States. There are about 30 species varying in color of petal and size.

6

Nasturtium *Tropaeolum*

Germinates in 2–3 weeks | Height varies

Species of nasturtium range from bushy to trailing and climbing varieties and are ideal for growing in hanging baskets. The bright jewel-colored flowers, leaves, and seedpods can be eaten (see page 36).

7

Shirley poppy *Papaver rhoeas*

Germinates in 1–2 weeks | 24 in (60 cm)

Developed from the basic red corn poppy with a black center, the blooms of Shirley poppies appear in white, red, and shades of pink and lilac with a white center and the petals look like crinkled silk.

8

Annual clary sage *Salvia viridis*

Germinates in 3 weeks | 24 in (60 cm)

Bees love to visit this bushy herb with soft, heart-shaped leaves and many flower spikes covered with tiny flowers. The spikes can be cut and dried out for long-lasting flower arrangements.

4

Candytuft *Iberis*

☀ 🌱 ◔ Germinates
in 3 weeks

▮ 10 in
(25 cm)

This plant originates from the
Mediterranean island of Crete, known
as "Candia" in old English. There are
varieties in shades of white, purple,
and red scented flowers that are
loved by butterflies.

5

Cornflower *Centaurea cyanus*

☀ 🌱 ◑ Germinates
in 2 weeks

▮ 12–18 in
(30–45 cm)

These annual plants produce bright
blue flowers with ruffled petals that
attract butterflies and bees. To have
flowers all through the summer, remove
any dying flowers or pick the flowers
to fill a vase to encourage more
to bloom.

9

Godetia *Clarkia amoena*

☀ 🌱 ◑ Germinates
in 2 weeks

▮ 16 in
(40 cm)

These plants are ideal for pots, since
they produce many multicolored
flowers with silky, wavy petals. They
can self-seed if the last flowers are
left to die, form seedpods, and release
their seeds.

10

Annual mallow *Lavatera trimestris*

☀ 🌱 ◑ Germinates
in 2–3 weeks

▮ 20 in
(50 cm)

Butterflies visit the strong jewel-like
pink or white flowers of this eye-
catching lavatera. The bushy plants
quickly grow upward and outward
throughout the summer.

Marigold fish

As one of the quickest- and easiest-to-grow flowers, marigolds are great for creating colorful containers. In this project, African marigolds have been grown with a smaller bedding plant, alyssum, to make a fun floral pattern.

Important stuff

Place container in full sunlight and use moist potting soil. The seeds germinate in 1 week and flowers appear 6 weeks later.

Top tip

Slugs love to eat marigold seedlings so protect the plants from them. See the advice on page 9.

1 **In a large** prepared container, use sand to mark out the outline of the shape of a goldfish on the moist soil.

2 **Sow the marigold** seeds 2 in (5 cm) apart within the fish shape. Cover the seeds lightly with soil by gently patting a strainer full of soil over them.

3 **Sprinkle the alyssum** seeds outside the fish shape and gently rake them into the soil. Water gently so as not to disturb the shape made by the seeds.

4 **Water the plants** regularly, especially during dry weather. Marigolds will grow to 6 in (15 cm) high to create the goldfish shape and the alyssum will grow smaller around them.

Floral shapes
gallery

Why not create some other shapes with flowers, such as your name, a machine or object, or a favorite animal?

Try using iberis to make a pet portrait.

Try using pansies to make the shape of a car.

Remove the dead flowers, since this will encourage further flowering.

Flowerpot people

Bright, sunny sunflowers look pretty in a pot. You can make them look even more cheerful by painting the pot and giving them a smiley face. For quick results, use dwarf sunflower seeds, but if you want to grow a pot person that's taller than you, use other varieties and a bigger pot.

Important stuff

Grow sunflowers in a place that gets full sun. Use well-drained soil. Seeds will germinate in 2-3 weeks and flowers will open after 7-10 weeks.

You will need:

5 quart (5 liter) cans or bigger

Enamel paints

Vaseline

Polyethylene bag

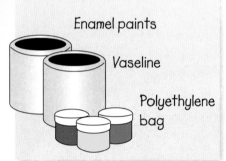

1 Draw the designs for the clothes of your flowerpot people on paper first, then use enamel paints to copy the designs onto some cans.

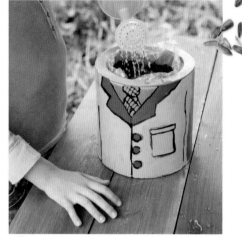

2 Ask an adult to make holes in the base of each can. Then spread some gravel on the bottom for drainage. Now fill the cans up with soil and water them well.

3 Make two holes ½ in (1.5 cm) deep near the center of each pot. Sow a seed in each hole and gently cover with soil. Cover the cans with a polyethylene bag with a few small holes in it.

4 Cover the sides of the cans with a ring of vaseline to deter slugs and position in a sunny spot. Remove the bags when the seedlings' leaves appear and remove the weaker plant.

5 Water little but often, since without water sunflowers will die quickly. If your flowers have more than one head developing, cut the extra ones later for an indoor flower display.

6 Once the sunflowers have opened, use a pencil or pointed stick to pick out some of the tiny flowers on the head to make a face. Eyes, noses, and mouths can be different shapes.

Sunflower gallery

From the Teddy bear to the Big smile, dwarf sunflower varieties are small and cheerful!

Ring of fire sunflower

Teddy bear sunflower

Pacino sunflower

Poppy power

The crinkled silky petals of poppies appear in a wonderful array of colors that attract bees and butterflies, and birds enjoy eating the seeds. Plan to sow the seeds in early spring for summer flowering or in early summer for fall flowering or for flowering the next spring.

Important stuff

Grow poppies in a place that gets full sun. Use poor, lightly moistened soil. Seeds will germinate in 2–4 weeks and flowers will open from 12 weeks onward.

1 **To begin, fill up** a prepared container with unfertilized soil. Poppies grow best in poor, lightly moistened soil. Make a shallow trench around the container using your finger.

2 **Sprinkle the seeds** into the trench and cover with a very little soil. Position the container in a sunny spot and keep the soil slightly moist until the shoots appear.

3 **Once the seedlings** appear, thin them to 4 in (10 cm) apart because overcrowded plants will become spindly without the room to branch out.

We've used seeds of the Iceland poppy variety.

4 **Water a little** only when the soil looks dry. Poppies like almost drought conditions so if it has rained in the week then they are likely not to need water.

Deadheading To lengthen the flowering period, remove the dead flowers by breaking the stalks a little way below them. This is called deadheading and encourages the plant to produce new flowers rather than spend its energy on producing seeds.

Poppy
gallery

There are over 120 species in the poppy family. Here are some of the best for containers:

Ladybug poppy

Top tip

Encourage reseeding for the next year by leaving some spent flowers at the end of the flowering period to form seedpods and letting the leaves die back.

California poppy

Iceland poppy

This takes 1 day.

Fairy ring

Grow a secret fairy ring in a hidden spot at the bottom of the yard. You never know, you might attract some fairies! A circle of ornamental grasses, along with delicate, sweet-smelling flowers, looks magical and makes a great place to play or have a picnic. Don't forget treats for the fairies!

You will need:

Ornamental grasses and a selection of unusually shaped flowers

Jars and glass paints or household paint and varnish

Tea light candles

Walk round, dragging the stick hard into the ground to mark the edge of the circle.

1 **Make a circular** area by sticking a plant stake where you'd like the middle of the ring to be. Tie a piece of string to this and tie another stake to the other end and use this to mark the edge.

2 **Use a shovel** to dig out a deep trench around the edge of the circle and sprinkle some potting soil into the base. Put the turf that you have taken out onto a compost heap.

Reuse the soil that was removed when digging the trench or use fresh soil.

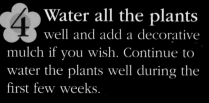

3 **Gently remove** each plant from its pot and place it into the trench. Fill soil around the plant's roots, pressing the soil down firmly to keep it upright.

4 **Water all the plants** well and add a decorative mulch if you wish. Continue to water the plants well during the first few weeks.

5 **Make pretty lanterns** by painting jars using special glass paint (or household paint and a layer of varnish). Place tea light candles inside the jars and ask an adult to light them in the evening.

Top tip

You could also add sparkly solar nightlights to light the fairy ring. They come on automatically at dusk.

When it rains, cover the jars with plastic.

Fairy ring
gallery

Look for mushroom fairy rings in nature, or create your own with small flowers. You can paint black fairy silhouettes on your lanterns, too.

Mushroom ring

Ring of crocuses

Fairy lantern

This takes 12 weeks.

Floral tepee

Morning glories are one of a number of climbing plants that quickly grow up and up if given a pole or trellis to climb. If you have the room, here is how to build a large flower-covered tepee—the perfect hideaway for summer games and adventures with friends.

Important stuff

Set up your tepee in a sheltered place that gets full sun. Keep soil moist. Morning glories grow to 6–8 ft (1.8–2.4 m) high. The seeds germinate in 2–3 weeks and flowers from 10 weeks.

You will need:

Morning glory seeds (soaked overnight)
Hazel beanpoles and dried-out branches
Sand
Large stones
Green wire or twine

1 **Mark out the base** of the tepee using sand or sticks.

2 **Every 1 ft (30 cm)** dig a large, deep hole around the marked line.

3 **Place a beanpole** into each hole and twist it into the ground, or push a large stone against it to stop the pole from wobbling.

4 **After filling the holes** with soil around the poles, ask an adult to bend the beanpoles together and use twine to tie them near the top.

5 **Use twine** to attach some dried-out branches, creating a doorway, windows, and interconnecting poles onto which the climbing plants can hook.

32

Top tip

Seeds can be germinated indoors for an early start, and the seedlings planted around the base of the tepee. Or buy seedlings from a garden center.

Cover with clear plastic bottles or containers to keep the seeds warm.

6 **Around** each beanpole, sprinkle a layer of seed compost, and then sow the seeds (which have been soaked overnight). Cover with a little more compost and water well.

7 **As the plants grow** up the beanpoles, wrap some growing tips around the dried branches so that a web of leaves and flowers is created.

8 **Keep the soil moist,** so water more during dry weather. Use a general liquid fertilizer once a month.

Sweet pea tepee

Alternatively, you could set up a mini-tepee in a container for your toys. Construct a frame using 4 to 6 poles and tying them together with twine at the top. Sow a couple of sweet pea seeds at the base of each pole in the early spring.

Cool plants to grow

Get ready to impress your friends with some unusual plants, from ones that look, smell, or feel strange to those with surprising behavior. Some can be grown from seed or bought from stores, while others can be started in some unusual ways.

1

Tickle-me plant *Mimosa pudica*

Germinates in 2-3 weeks · 12 in (30 cm)

When touched, the fernlike leaves of this very sensitive plant curl up, setting off a chain reaction where nearby leaf stalks of the plant fold in, too. The leaves also fold over in the dark. If touched too many times, the plant's reaction may slow down.

2

Coleus *Coleus blumei*

Germinates in 2 weeks · Dwarf and tall varieties

Grown indoors or outdoors, this eye-catching plant has dramatic, colorful leaves. Encourage the plant to become bushy and last longer by pinching out the small flowers and growing shoots at the end of summer.

3

This seedling is ready to be planted into soil.

Avocado pit *Persea americana*

Germinates in 6 weeks · Very tall tree

Impress yourself as well as your friends by growing your own avocado plant from its pit. Push three toothpicks into the center of the pit (pointed end upward), and place over a jar full of water so that the pit dips in. A seedling will form.

6

Ornamental gourds *Curcurbita pepo*

Germinates in 2 weeks · Height varies

There's an impressive array of strangely shaped, colored, and patterned gourds to choose from. In the fall, they can be dried to make interesting hanging decorations or the larger gourds can be hollowed out to become interesting plant containers.

7

Pineapple top *Ananas comosus*

Rooting: in 6-8 weeks · 12 in (30 cm)

Slice the leafy top off a fresh pineapple, strip away a few leaves at the base, leave to dry, and then place into a pot with potting soil and keep moist. Hey presto—within six weeks the top starts to root! Although it will be a year or two before it fruits.

8

Chocolate cosmos *Cosmos atrosanguineus*

Germinates in 5-10 days · 3 ft (90 cm)

The dark brown-red flowers of this perennial plant produce a powerful smell of vanilla and sweet chocolate. Originally from Mexico, the plant is no longer found in the wild. The blooms last through the summer and into the fall.

4

Lablab beans *Lablab purpureus*

Germinates in 2-3 weeks | 6 ft (2m)

Lablab beans are climbing plants that produce pods that can be eaten when cooked. They have stunning purple and pink fragrant flowers, followed by fascinating dark purple seedpods, surrounded by green and purple-brown leaves.

5

Corn (maize) *Zea mays*

Germinates in 1-2 weeks | 5 ft (1.5 m)

Sow some corn seeds bought from a pet store or garden center into a container about 4 in (10 cm) apart and, if kept moist, fertilized, and warm, in about 3 months corncobs will be ready to harvest. It's a-maize-ing!

9

Venus flytrap *Dionaea muscipula*

Germinates in 4-6 weeks | 6 in (15 cm)

Venus flytraps survive by feeding on flies and other insects. They are fascinating to watch for their reactions. You could feed your plant, using tweezers to place an insect inside its head-trap every 10 days. Avoid touching the trigger hairs.

10

Lemon verbena *Alpysia triphylla*

Germinates in 2-3 weeks | A bushy shrub

If you rub your fingers on the leaves of the lemon verbena plant, they will pick up a powerful smell of lemon. On page 70, we've used these leaves to flavor herbal teas. They can also be added to potpourris. New plants can be grown by taking cuttings.

Nasturtium nibbles

Important stuff

These grow best in full sun and in poor, dry soil. Their height varies depending on the variety. The seeds germinate in 1–2 weeks and flowers appear 6 weeks later.

Are nasturtiums a flower or a vegetable? They're both! Their brightly colored flowers and shield-shaped leaves can all be eaten. So grow them in a hanging basket and surprise your friends by casually picking a leaf or two (rinse them under the faucet) and popping them in your mouth.

You will need:

A bag with hanging straps
Nasturtium seeds
Slow-release fertilizer
A plastic garbage bag
Potting soil

The Latin name for water cress is *Nasturtium*, and it can also be eaten. See page 50 to find out how to grow it at home.

1 **First, prepare the bag** by lining it with a garbage bag. Next, use scissors to snip holes in the base for water drainage. Snip through both the bag and the lining.

2 **Mix some potting soil** with a slow-release fertilizer and fill the basket almost to the brim, ready to sow the seed. Water the soil and let it drain through.

4 **About a week later,** little green shield-shaped leaves will poke their way through the soil. Give them a drink of water.

5 **When several leaves** have appeared and the bright flowers bloom, they are ready to eat. It's time to harvest the crop!

Collect the seeds when the flowers have died and store them until they are hard and dry. Keep them in an airtight container in a cool dry place and remember to label them. You can then plant them for next year's crop.

Remember: Ask an adult before eating things from the garden!

3 **Make a number** of ½ in (1 cm) deep holes, 4 in (10 cm) apart, around the basket and in the center. Place a seed into each hole and cover with soil.

Make flowery ice cubes by putting flowers into an ice cube tray with water, then freeze.

6 **Add a few nasturtium leaves** and flowers to a mixed leaf salad. If you leave some flowers on the stalks, they will form tiny wrinkled seeds. You can eat these, too!

Top tip

Nasturtiums need little attention and prefer the soil to be kept fairly dry. However, in a hanging basket or bag, the soil can dry out quickly, so water regularly, especially in dry weather.

Window-box wildlife

Secure your crate to a sunny window ledge.

Opening the curtains in the morning will be a whole new experience with bees, ladybugs, and butterflies flocking to your window box. Make your visitors feel at home with colorful flowers, lots of hiding places, and a nice drink of water.

1 **If you are using** a wooden crate, line with plastic and cut holes to prevent the wood from rotting. Place rocks over the holes in the base and fill the container ¾ full with soil.

2 **First arrange** the plants, then make deep holes and place them in. Finally, fill in around the plant with soil, making sure the base of the stem where it meets the root is level with the soil's surface.

3 **Water the plants** well to help them settle in. Make sure space has been left at the top of the container so that the soil won't spill over when watering or during heavy rain.

Use a flat stone to weigh the bottle down at the front end.

4 **Make a mini ladybug house** by folding some corrugated cardboard inside a bottle. Tilt the bottle downward among the plants to prevent water from getting inside.

5 **Add a small dish** or foil tray, sinking it into the soil. Fill it with water and place some small flat stones around the edge to create a tiny pond.

6 **Tie together** some hollow sticks and dried seedpods for creatures to crawl into, and add a rock or two for them to crawl under. Once completed, place the window box on a flat surface.

We used lavender, chives, snapdragons, hebe, and ivy. These will attract busy bees and fluttering butterflies—all great pollinators. Lacewings and ladybugs will eat up any pesky aphids. Many other beetles, and maybe a spider or two, may also drop by to pay you a visit.

Snapdragon

Dwarf hebe

Chives

Ivy

Lavender

Wild-West cacti

Yee-hah! Turn a container into a desert landscape by filling it with prickly cacti and other succulents. Because they store water in their fleshy leaves, stems, or roots, succulents can survive in harsh conditions such as deserts, scrublands, and mountains.

Horticultural sand   Perlite   Peat-based potting soil

Most cacti and succulents need soil that lets water drain away quickly to stop the plants from rotting. So use either a cactus potting mix, or create your own using peat-based potting soil and coarse sand in equal amounts. Add some perlite or vermiculite, since these also allow for quick draining.

Cover your cacti with clear plastic bottles or containers to keep them warm.

1 **Sprinkle a thin layer** of gravel into a seed tray. Most cacti have shallow roots, since they store water in their stems. Add 1–2 in (2–5 cm) of cactus potting mix, and make holes for the plants.

2 **Beginning with the** largest cactus, ease each plant gently out of its old container. To do this, wear gloves and use tongs or wrap the cactus in newspaper, paper towels, or light cardboard.

3 **Place the first cactus** into its hole and use the back of a spoon to press the soil down around its base. Transplant the rest of the plants in the same way.

4 **Mist the soil or** sprinkle it lightly with lukewarm water. Repeat after the potting mix has looked very dry for a few days.

5 **Add details to make** your landscape look like the Wild West. Create a track using sand or gravel, for example, and add model cowboys and Indians.

Place your landscape in a warm, partly shaded site.

This is a hairy trumpet cactus.

Pets' corner

Why not grow some tasty treats for your pets? Cats, dogs, guinea pigs, and rabbits love to nibble plants, but it's important to provide them with ones they can safely eat. The grasses grown here provide nutrition for your pets as well.

Important stuff

Grow in a sunny place and use well-drained soil. The seeds germinate within 1-2 weeks and the grasses are ready to be nibbled after 4 weeks.

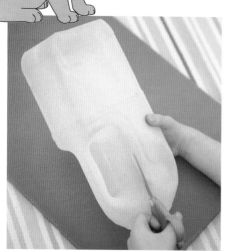

1 **For the labels,** cut a panel from a plastic milk carton and then draw an outline of the shape of your pet with a black marker.

2 **Add features,** such as whiskers, eyes, nose, and a mouth, using the black marker. Then cut out the pet shape so it's ready as a label for the container.

3 **For each container,** ask an adult to drill some holes in the base. Fill with a little gravel and then add potting soil. Moisten the soil and let the water soak through.

4 **If the seeds are large,** such as cat grass for cats, push them slightly below the surface and then cover them with soil using your fingertips.

5 **If the seeds are small,** such as Lucerne grass for dogs, sprinkle them over the surface of the moist soil and add a thin layer of soil on top.

6 **Keep the containers** well watered as the plants grow. Trim the plants using scissors to keep them at a good height for your pet.

Cat grass for your cat

Lucerne grass
for your dog

For other pets . . .

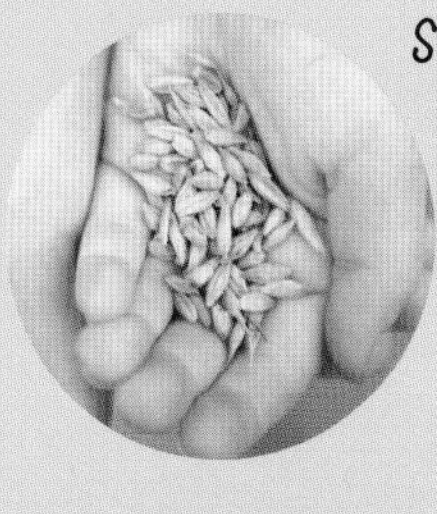

Sow barley, oats,
and wheat for
your rabbit.

Rabbit

Sow timothy
meadow grass and
plantains for your
guinea pigs.

Guinea pig

Ready set grow!

Vegetables, herbs, and fruits

Growing your own food is a rewarding and impressive achievement, and you'll be amazed at just how quickly you can start eating what you grow. Sprouting seeds can be eaten within a few days, microgreens eaten within a week, and some crops are fully grown within a month. Try out new tastes, such as kohl rabi and Chinese vegetables, grow a pizza garden, and make herbal teas warmed up by the sun and a refreshing red currant drink for those hot summer days.

Make labels from one side of a plastic milk bottle and write on the date started.

12 weeks to go!

Start Strawberry boot on page 72
Start Carrot companions on page 62
Start Colorful kebabs on page 66

9 weeks to go!

Start Crazy kohl rabi on page 58

6 weeks to go!

Tip: When transplanting a seedling, water it first, water into the planting hole, and water it again after planting.

3 weeks to go!

Look for herbs in a garden center.

Countdown to harvesting

11 weeks to go!

Use a homemade propagator on page 6 to get your seeds germinating.

Always make holes in the base of your container to allow excess water to seep out.

10 weeks to go!

Start Magic beans on page 68

Choose colorful dwarf bean seeds.

8 weeks to go!

Tip: Thin out seedlings to stop overcrowding and to prevent the young plants from getting diseases. See page 8 to find out how you can protect your plants from pests.

7 weeks to go!

Radishes only take 4 weeks to grow!

5 weeks to go!

Start Pizza garden on page 64

4 weeks to go!

Start Windowsill watercress on page 50
Start Radish racers on page 52
Start Salad relay on page 54
Start Taste of Asia on page 60

2 weeks to go!

Check out the top 10 microgreens on page 56. They are ready to eat in two weeks.

1 week to go!

Start One-week sprouters on page 46
Start Herbal sun tea on page 70
Start Red currant refreshments on page 74

One-week sprouters

Sprouts are seeds that have *just* begun to germinate, so you can grow them in only a few days. They're tasty and nutty and crunchy—and very good for you, so nibble them by the handful or sprinkle them on salads and sandwiches. We've used snow peas, one of many edible sprouting seeds (see page 48). There are two main ways to germinate seeds quickly.

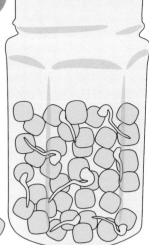

Method 1:

1 **Place a few sheets** of paper towels onto a shallow tray and soak in water. Spread your seeds over the damp surface and place the tray in a warm place— like in front of a sunny window.

2 **Keep the paper towel** moist at all times and watch the seeds germinate. Taste them after a few days, but eat them over the next five days.

Method 2:

We used the toe end of a clean pair of panty hose instead of muslin.

1 **Put two tablespoons** of seeds into a large glass jar. Fill it ¾ full of water and cover with a piece of clean muslin. Secure with a rubber band and leave for 8-12 hours, or overnight.

2 **Drain the water away** through the muslin, then rinse the seeds with cold water and drain well again. Place the jar on a warm windowsill out of direct sunlight.

3 **Rinse and drain the** seeds with cold water twice a day. After a couple of days, taste a few sprouts to see if they are ready to eat.

4 **When the sprouts are** ready, rinse and drain them for a final time, then take off the muslin and leave them for eight hours so all the water can dry off.

You will need:

Snow pea seeds
and either:
Paper towels
Shallow tray
or:
Empty glass jar
Clean muslin or
toe end of clean
panty hose
Rubber band

To make a simple, scrumptious, and super-healthy wrap, tuck a handful of sprouting seeds, a slice of ham, and a lettuce leaf inside a wrap.

Top tip

Store your seeds in the refrigerator so they don't become moldy, and make sure to eat them within five days.

Top 10 Sprouting seeds

Here are some more sprouts to grow and eat. See page 46 for how to grow these tasty and healthy snacks in just a few days. Sow a new batch each week and you can be munching on them all year round. There are many seeds to choose from, but here is our top 10.

See page 46

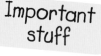

Important stuff

All sprouts need a warm place to grow. Keep the seeds in a dark place if you want white sprouts, or keep them on a sunny windowsill for green sprouts. They will taste slightly different.

1

Alfalfa *Medicago sativa*

Harvest in 2-6 days

Alfalfa sprouts taste crispy and crunchy. This plant is also known as Lucerne grass, which is harvested as hay for cattle and is nibbled as grass by dogs (see page 42).

(see page 42)

2

Chickpea *Cicer arietinum*

Harvest in 2-4 days

The nutty, mild taste of chickpea sprouts makes these sprouts a popular ingredient in many Asian dishes. The chickpea plant has been grown by farmers for over 7,500 years and was eaten by prehistoric people.

3

Mung beans *Vigna radiata*

Harvest in 4-6 days

Also known as Chinese bean sprouts, mung beans along with other sprouts are great for adding to stir-fries. They sprout from small oval green beans that are light yellow inside.

6

Beet sprouting seeds *Beta vulgaris*

Harvest in 3-6 days

These seeds come from a leafy vegetable with swollen red roots known as a beet. The dramatic red sprouts have a mild beet taste.

7

Mustard and cress *Brassica hirta* and *Lepidium sativum*

Harvest in 7 days

Try these spicy, peppery sprouts if you are looking for a flavor with a bit of zing. You could sow them on the top of moist cotton stuffed inside an empty eggshell. Draw a face onto the shell. As the seeds grow, they'll look like a wacky hair style.

8

Green peas *Pisum sativum*

Harvest in 2-3 days

These are the peas found inside the seedpods of pea plants and are also known as garden peas. The tender, leafy shoots have a sweet taste.

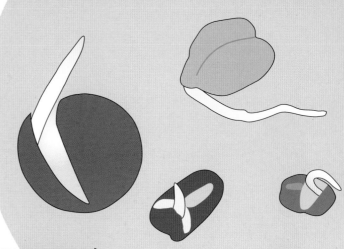

4

Lentils *Lens culinaris*

☼ ◔ Harvest in 2-4 days

Lentils are the flat oval seeds from the pods of a bushy pea-related plant and come in a range in colors, including yellow, orange, green, and black. The sprouts have a nutty, peppery taste and are a great source of iron. You can use the ones sold for cooking.

5

Azuki beans *Vigna angularis*

○ ◔ Harvest in 4-8 days

Popular in Japanese cooking, these dark red beans pale in color as they soak. The sprouts have a strong nutty, sweet taste.

9

Snow peas   *Pisum sativum* var. *macrocarpon*

☼ ◑ Harvest in 2-10 days

Snow peas come from the sugar-pod type of pea plant where the whole pod can be eaten. The sprouts have the top set of leaves of the pea plant and taste sweeter than green pea sprouts.

10

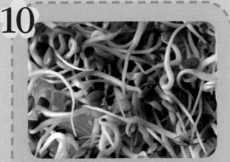

Fenugreek *Trigonella foenum-graecum*

☼ ◔ Harvest in 2-4 days

Those who enjoy spicy curry dishes should try the shoots of strong-smelling fenugreek seeds. Before turning green, these yellow sprouts are used as a spice, added to flavor tea, mixed with yogurt as a conditioner for hair, and used in medicine.

Windowsill watercress

Garnish your food with tasty, shiny, watercress leaves—or make a yummy salad with watercress as the main attraction. This super-healthy plant is full of many of the vitamins and minerals that your body needs and will help to keep you in tip-top shape.

Important stuff

Watercress grows in full sun. Keep the soil moist. The plants grow 6–20 in (15–50 cm) high over 4 weeks or more.

Did you know?

Hippocrates, an ancient Greek doctor (known as the "father of medicine"), built the world's first hospital. He chose a spot next to a stream of spring water so he could grow fresh watercress for his patients to eat.

Never pick wild watercress—it may contain a waterborne parasite called a liver fluke.

1 **Fill a recycled** container (put holes in its base first) ¾ full of seed compost. Place it onto a plastic tray and wet the soil, using a plastic bottle with a few holes in its lid as a spray.

2 **Sprinkle watercress** seeds over the surface of the seed compost and gently press them into the soil. Cover the container while the seeds germinate.

3 **The soil needs to be** kept moist at all times, so make sure there's always water in the plastic tray. Tap water contains many of the minerals watercress needs to grow.

4 **After 4 weeks, snip** the top shoots off with a pair of scissors. If you do this, the plants will regrow quickly and become bushier. Always wash watercress well before eating it.

Top tip

The secret of growing watercress is to keep the soil damp, but make sure it's never saturated, since overwatering can kill your crop!

Cress cuttings

Another way to grow watercress is to start from cuttings.

1 Place some long shoots from a bag of supermarket watercress into a container of water.

2 In the water, the cuttings will develop roots, and new shoots will begin to grow.

3 When the cuttings have developed lots of roots, repot them into moist potting soil.

51

This takes 4 weeks.

Radish racers

Did you know that radishes are related to cabbages and cauliflowers? Grown for thousands of years, these cheerful root vegetables are super quick to germinate. Eaten whole or chopped up in salads, they have a crunchy texture and a delightfully peppery taste—and they're packed with vitamins!

Important stuff

Radishes grow in sunny or partly shaded places. Keep the soil moist. The roots are ready to harvest a month after planting.

Day 1

1 **Make sure there are** no large lumps in your soil, and plant the seeds about 1 in (3 cm) apart, and around ½ in (1 cm) deep.

Week 2

2 **Once your radishes** have germinated, keep an eye on them, since you may have to thin them out. Make sure the soil is well watered, especially in dry weather.

Week 3

3 **You'll be surprised** how quickly your radishes develop. If conditions are just right, they can be fully grown in about 18 days.

Week 4

Radishes sown in the summer months will need more watering and care.

4 **Your radishes will** probably be ready to harvest in three to four weeks. It's best to eat them soon—they'll turn woody if you leave them too long.

Repeat sowing It's a good idea to sow radishes at intervals of about 10 days, so you get a continuous crop to harvest. In fact, it's best to sow only a few radishes at a time, since they don't keep and taste best as soon as they mature. If you find your radishes taste a bit too peppery, try peeling them before eating them—most of the strong taste is in the skin.

PEST PATROL

Radish leaves are often attacked by slugs, and they are also vulnerable to flea beetles, known for their jumping ability. It helps to keep the crop watered, since flea beetles like dry conditions.

Radish gallery

Radishes come in a huge number of varieties and lots of different colors and sizes.

Chinese daikon radish

French breakfast radishes

Easter egg radishes

Springtime radishes

53

This takes **4** weeks.

Salad relay

Salad leaves grow quickly, and when you cut them, new ones form. If you sow lots of plants at the same time, they'll all be ready together, and you'll have salad leaves coming out of your ears. Instead, try sowing a row every two weeks to provide a steady supply.

Important stuff

Salad leaves grow in full sun and most soil types are suitable. The seeds germinate in 1 week and the leaves are ready to harvest from 3 weeks.

Week 1

1 Set up a planter and put a thin layer of gravel in the base. Fill it with potting soil and water it well, then wait for the water to drain through, leaving the soil moist.

2 Make a ½ in (1 cm) deep trench along the back of the planter and sow seeds thinly along it. Brush soil over them lightly with your fingertips. Water using a watering can.

Week 2

3 Two weeks later, thin the first seedlings so your plants have room to grow. Make another trench in the middle of the planter, sow more seeds thinly, and cover them lightly with soil.

Week 3

Week 4

4 The first leaves will be ready to eat after about three weeks. Use scissors to cut about 1 in (2.5 cm) above the base of the stem, leaving a stump that will grow into more leaves.

5 After a further week, make another trench along the front of the planter and sow a third row. Thin the seedlings of the second row and continue to cut the leaves from the first row of plants.

For a continuous supply through the summer, start a second planter. After a few croppings, replace the soil from the first planter so the relay can continue...

PEST PATROL

Cover your planter with fine mesh netting to protect the seedlings from pests such as birds, slugs, and snails. This netting will also prevent butterflies from laying their eggs, which hatch into hungry caterpillars. To keep your planter away from slugs and snails, place it on a tabletop, a windowsill, or even a couple of bricks, rather than putting it on the ground.

Label each row with a marker made from one side of a plastic milk bottle and write the date on it when the row was sown.

Top tip
Throughout the relay, keep your crops well watered, especially when the weather is dry, to prevent the plants from bolting (flowering and producing seeds).

Keep the relay going, cutting small leaves when they're 3 or 4 weeks old, or, if you want larger leaves, cutting from 4 weeks onward.

Microgreens

Join in the new trend of growing and eating microgreens. These tasty and very healthy seedlings are the next stage on from the sprouts and their appearance livens up a salad. They are ready to eat within 7–14 days, when the first true leaves appear, and are simply grown on a moist layer of cotton balls, felt, or potting soil in a shallow container on a warm windowsill and watered daily.

1

Broccoli

The seedlings of broccoli have a slightly strong, spicy taste. Broccoli is one of the healthiest foods to eat. Its name comes from a Latin word meaning branch or arm.

2

Arugula

Arugula is a member of the mustard family. With long, bright green leaves on slender white stems, the seedlings have a mild peppery, nutty taste. These can be added to garnish pizzas and pastas.

3

Red beet

The green leaf tops and deep red stems of red beet will brighten up a bowl of salad. They taste juicy just like a fully grown beet and are full of goodness to keep us healthy.

6

Red cabbage

The red cabbage seedlings have pale red stems and heart-shaped green leaves. They taste like mild cabbages. Also try growing seedlings of white and green cabbages.

7

Spinach

Originally grown in the Middle East and then brought to Europe via Spain, spinach comes in three varieties—the curly savoy, the flat-leaf smooth variety, and the semi savoy, which is not as curly. The seedlings have rich green leaves that taste milder than mature spinach.

8

Rapini

Rapini is known by many names around the world, including broccoli raab, but the plant is related to turnips, not broccoli. The seedlings taste slightly bitter, similar to the mustardlike leaves of white turnips.

4

Cilantro

Also known as fresh coriander or Chinese parsley, the young leaves of cilantro are not only used to garnish salads and exotic main dishes but also to flavor soups and sauces.

5

Swiss chard

Swiss chard has colored stems and green leaves with a mild sweet taste. Look for varieties with dramatic red and yellow stems to grow.

9

Corn salad

Also known as lamb's lettuce, mâche, and rapunzel, corn salad contains three times as much vitamin C as lettuce. It is so-called because farmers found it growing in cornfields. The small rosettes of leaves have a slightly nutty taste.

10

Celery

The crunchy leaves and mild taste of the seedlings are similar to the mature celery plant. During ancient times, physicians used celery to treat many ailments, since it contains lots of goodness.

Important stuff

Grow on a warm windowsill on a moist layer of cotton balls, felt, or potting soil. ready to pick when 1-2 in (2.5-5 cm) high, which takes 1-2 weeks.

After picking, the moistened seedlings can be sealed in a plastic bag and kept in the fridge for up to five days.

Crazy kohl rabi

Important stuff

Kohl rabi grows in a sunny place and in rich, well-drained soil. The seeds germinate in 7–10 days and the kohl rabi are ready to be picked 7–8 weeks later.

If you come across a weird vegetable that looks like cabbage leaves growing out of a turnip, you'll have found a kohl rabi ("cabbage turnip" in German). It's crunchy with a nutty taste a bit like cabbage and broccoli, but milder. Fairly quick to grow, it's becoming very popular in Europe.

1 Set up your container (choose something very deep) using the self-irrigation system that's described on page 10.

2 Fill the container with soil, making sure some goes into the small plastic container in the base. Moisten the soil and allow the water to drain away.

3 Sprinkle seeds around the container and sift a fine layer of soil on top. Water the soil lightly again and cover it using a plastic bag with holes in it.

Bring the container under cover if it's going to rain heavily.

Cover the container with fine insect mesh or a net curtain to prevent butterflies and cabbage-root fly from laying eggs on the plants. The mesh also protects the plants from birds.

4 Once the seedlings appear, remove the plastic bag so you can thin them out. To grow to a healthy size, they should be about 4 in (10 cm) apart.

5 For watering, pour the water through the pipe until it begins to fill, since this means the reservoir is full. From time to time, check the water level—if you can't see it, refill it.

6 Harvest kohl rabi when it's still young— between the size of a golf ball and a tennis ball. If it's left too long, it will lose its flavor and the texture will be tough and woody.

Kohl rabi varieties have either purple or greenish-white skin. Once the skin has been peeled away, however, they look and taste similar. The round white bulbs can be eaten raw or cooked. They can be grated onto salads, cut into stir-fry slivers, diced into soup, or boiled to accompany a main dish.

For this recipe, you will need:

1 kohl rabi bulb, peeled
1 green apple, cored
2 tablespoons honey
1 tablespoon olive oil
Zest and juice of half a lemon
Two handfuls of cashew nuts and walnuts
A handful of soft cheese cubes

Cool kohl salad

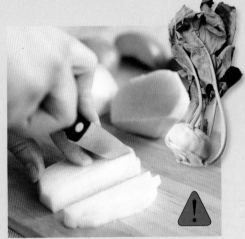

1 **Slice the kohl rabi** and the apples into thin strips.

2 **Mix the zest** and juice of the lemon with the honey and olive oil to make the dressing.

3 **Toast the cashews** and walnuts in a pan. Toss all the ingredients together and add the cheese. Leave for 5 minutes so the dressing can soften the kohl rabi, then serve.

Top tip

Kohl rabi leaves can be eaten too if they look firm and green. Boil them like cabbage, but use them soon after picking. You can store the kohl rabi bulb for a week unwashed in the refrigerator.

Taste of Asia

Zap up a salad or add zing to a stir-fry using the baby leaves and stems of vegetables originally from China, Japan, and other East Asian countries. From the milder taste of pak choi to the peppery mustard greens, Asian vegetables are ready to be picked again and again within a month of sowing.

Important stuff

Grow in full sun or part shade with an even amount of light. Use rich compost and keep the soil moist. The seeds germinate in 1–2 weeks and the leaves are ready to pick within 30 days.

1 **Ask an adult** to prepare a couple of boxes by putting in a garbage bag and punching holes through the bag and the base. Fill the boxes with a little gravel for drainage and then potting soil, leaving a space at the top. Moisten the soil.

2 **Use a finger** to make a ½ in (1 cm) deep trench across the box. This could be in a looped shape or in straight lines.

3 **Sow the seeds thinly** into the trench. Use a sprinkler watering can to water without disturbing the seeds. Cover the box with a clear polyethylene bag during germination.

Bolting

In dry weather, these plants need to be kept well watered. Otherwise, they will stop producing delicious leaves and put all their energy into flowering and producing seeds to complete their life cycle before they die. This stage in a leafy vegetable's life is called bolting. Spring is the best time to grow these plants before the weather gets hot.

Thinnings

4 **Once the seedlings** appear, remove the cover and thin out so there's about a 2 in (5 cm) gap between each plant. The thinnings can be eaten.

5 **Water well** as the plants grow to keep them from bolting when dry. After 30 days, pick a few young leaves from each plant to encourage new growth.

Asian greens gallery

Asian vegetables have unusual and interestingly shaped leaves. Their seeds can be found in individual packets or in a mixed selection.

Pak choi

Mibuna and mizuna

Chinese mustard greens

Japanese mustard spinach (Komatsuna)

PEARL RIVER BRIDGE
SUPERIOR LIGHT
SOY SAUCE
生抽王
500mLX12

Naturally Brewed
According to HACCP, ISO9001, ISO14001

A programme of random sampling and analysis (accredited to the ISO17025 standard), demonstrates that all batches of PRB soy sauce tested within this programme have been below the EU legislative limit specified for 3-MCPD.

Dish up a stir-fry

Add your homegrown Asian greens to a stir-fry!

Heat up a tablespoon of sesame oil in a wok, then throw in handfuls of Asian ingredients. Stir for a minute or so, then pour over a little soy sauce and serve with a bowlful of noodles.

You will need:

Pak choi and Chinese chives

Bean sprouts

Tatsoi and Chinese mustard

Soy sauce

Sesame oil

Peanut shoots

Pine nuts

61

Carrot companions

Did you know that gardeners purposely grow some plants together to help produce the healthiest crops? This is called companion planting. Leeks, onions, or garlic are useful companions to carrots, since their strong smell keeps away flies that attack carrots.

Grow carrots and leeks in a sunny or partly shaded place and use well-drained, light soil. The seeds will germinate in 3 weeks and they will be ready to harvest in 12 weeks.

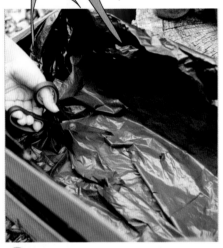

1 **Line a deep crate** with a garbage bag, cut to fit, and make a few small holes through the crate and the bag with scissors. Spread out a layer of gravel in the bottom for drainage.

2 **Mix a bucketful of potting soil** with sand and then fill up the crate. Moisten the soil before sowing the seed.

3 **Make three trenches** that are ½ in (1 cm) deep along the length of crate using a ruler or a stick.

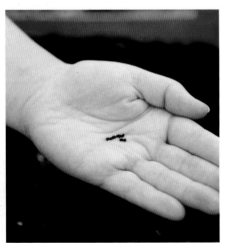

5 **Sow salad leek seeds** individually 6 in (15 cm) apart into the middle trench.

6 **Put in sticks** along the edges to hold up a polyethylene bag cover. This will encourage germination. The cover should be removed once the seedlings appear.

7 **If needed, thin** the carrot seedlings to ½ in (1 cm) between the plants to allow the carrots to form larger roots. Water well during dry weather.

PEST PATROL

During the summer,
low-flying female carrot flies are
attracted to the smell of carrots
and lay their eggs at the base of
them. Gardeners protect their carrots by:
• companion planting with onions, leeks, and garlic.
• covering them under a horticultural fleece.
• surrounding them with a fine netting 2 ft (60 cm) high
or growing them in tall pots.
• using carrot varieties that have some resistance to
carrot fly, such as Flyaway, Maestro, Sytan, and Resistafly.

4 **Sprinkle baby carrot**
seeds along the outer trenches
and cover them with a little soil. If
you space out the seeds, there will
be no need for thinning later,
which releases a carrot smell.

8 **Harvest the carrots**
and leeks when they reach a
good size. If the leeks need longer
then leave them in the container
until the winter when they have
thickened up.

Top tip
Sow the carrot seeds
in late spring to miss
the first invasion of
carrot flies.

Pizza garden

Growing a pizza takes a bit longer than ordering in, but the results are much yummier AND much healthier. In early summer, buy small tomato and pepper plants, onions, and Italian herbs, and transplant them into a container. Soon they'll be ready to pick, prepare, and eat.

Important stuff

All these plants like full sun. Grow them in rich, moist soil. Once the flowers appear on the tomato and pepper plants, feed every 2 weeks with a tomato fertilizer.

You will need:

3 vegetables: dwarf pepper and tomato plants, and onion sets
3 herbs: basil, thyme, and oregano plants
6 polystyrene pizza bases
Large round container

1 **Make a pretty edge** on six polystyrene pizza bases and decorate with acrylic paint. Then cut a flat edge across each plate so they can all slot into your container as section dividers.

Make slots in the soil first so your dividers won't break.

2 **Drill holes in the** base of a round container, add stones for drainage, and fill it with potting soil, leaving a space at the top. Using your pizza bases, divide the circle into six sections.

Hold the root ball and not the leaves or stem.

4 **If the plant's roots** are packed tightly together (because they've been in a small pot for too long), try to tease them apart with your fingertips. Do this very gently—tiny roots are delicate!

5 **Place the plant** in the hole. The crown of the plant (the base of the stem) should be level with the soil surface. Fill in the soil around the roots and press it down firmly, then water.

6 **Arrange the tomato,** basil, dwarf pepper, thyme, salad onion, and oregano plants in the sections. For the best effect when the plants are grown, alternate herbs with vegetables.

Perfect pizza!

Ask an adult to help you make a pizza base—or buy one. Spread tomato sauce over the top and add some grated cheese. Now chop up and add all your fresh ingredients and bake in a hot oven. Enjoy!

If the tomato and pepper plants begin to flop, push a plant stake into the soil near the stem and tie them together loosely. To do this, use string in a figure-eight loop so the stem doesn't rub against the stake.

3 **For each plant,** make a deep hole in the soil large enough for the root ball. Water the plant, then remove it from its pot by squeezing the sides or poking a finger through the hole.

7 **Once the plants** are in, place your container in a sunny spot. Be sure to soak it well from time to time—to do this, pour in water right up to the rim, filling the space you left above the soil.

Colorful kebabs

Jewel-bright skewers of vegetables make an ideal summer snack. Zucchinis are a winner for being one of the quickest—and easiest—members of the squash family to grow. Your plants can normally produce lots, too, so you'll have plenty to give away.

Important stuff

Grow in full sun and use moist, rich seed compost. The plants will grow to about 2 ft (60 cm) high. The seeds germinate in 1 week and the zucchinis are ready to harvest in 12 weeks.

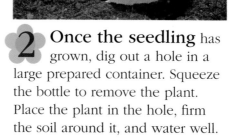

Cover the propagator with a small container that has holes poked through it to create the ideal germinating conditions.

1 **Use a propagator** (see page 7) to grow your seeds in. Make a ½ in (1.5 cm) deep hole, then push two seeds (on their sides) into the hole. When the seedlings appear, pull out the weakest one.

2 **Once the seedling** has grown, dig out a hole in a large prepared container. Squeeze the bottle to remove the plant. Place the plant in the hole, firm the soil around it, and water well.

3 **Add mulch** around the plant (see page 11 for ideas) to help the soil stay moist and weed-free. Make sure the mulch doesn't touch the stem.

A fungus called powdery mildew can appear on zucchini plant leaves. Prevent this by keeping your plants well-watered, fed, and with space around them for good air-flow.

4 **A zucchini plant** needs constantly moist soil, so bury a 6 in (15 cm) pot that has holes in its base next to the plant. Frequently water into the pot so that it will flow directly to the roots.

5 **When the first flowers** begin to form, feed the plant every 10–14 days with a tomato fertilizer and some compost tea (see page 9). Do not overfeed though.

6 **When the zucchinis** are 4 in (10 cm) long, cut them at their base. This will encourage more zucchinis to grow on your plant.

Top tip

Another good recipe is to grate zucchini and mix the gratings with whisked up egg, onion, and grated cheese. Fry the mixture in a frying pan until light brown on both sides.

Create a kebab

Planning a barbecue, or need a tasty side dish? Then try out this colorful kebab.

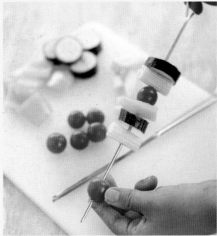

1 **Carefully** thread some slices of yellow pepper, zucchini, baby corn, and some cherry tomatoes onto some skewers or kebab sticks.

2 **Using a pastry brush,** baste the vegetables with some olive oil before placing them onto a griddle or barbecue, or under the grill. Watch them and ask an adult to turn them over a few times during cooking so that the vegetables will brown all over.

Magic beens

Green ones, yellow ones, purple ones—who knew there was magic in a bucket of beans? The magic is the sparkling assortment of colors, shapes, and sizes of bean variety just waiting for you to grow. For quick results, start with dwarf French bean seeds.

Important stuff

Choose a sunny place that is sheltered from the wind. Use rich, well-drained potting soil. Dwarf beans grow 20 in (50 cm) high. The seeds germinate in 7-10 days and the beans are ready to pick in 10 weeks.

1 Decorate a black bucket with stars cut out from foil food containers. Stick on the stars with any strong, quick-drying glue that is suitable for plastic.

2 Buy a few varieties of dwarf French bean seeds to produce different colored beans. We used dwarf green, purple king, and yellow rocquencourt beans.

3 Soak the beans overnight to encourage them to germinate. After soaking, the seeds will have begun to swell.

Put newspaper underneath the bucket to catch any spilt glitter.

4 Make a few 2 in (5 cm) deep holes spaced equally around the soil-filled bucket, and put a soaked bean into each hole. Fill the hole with soil and cover with a bag.

5 Spread glue on the bucket's lip and cover it with glitter to keep slugs away from the seedlings. For extra protection, sprinkle glitter, broken eggshells, or crushed seashells on the soil.

6 When the seedlings appear, cut both ends off some plastic bottles and use them to protect each one from slugs. Keep the plants well watered as they grow.

7 **Tying the plant stems** to plant stakes or twiggy branches stops them from falling over. Use a figure-eight loop so the stems don't rub against the supports. Keep well watered.

8 **Check under** the leaves for aphids. Remove them by wrapping tape around your fingers (sticky side out) and rubbing them off, or spraying them with water to knock them off.

9 **Pick the beans** when they're about 4 in (10 cm) long, before they mature and become too tough to eat. This also encourages more to grow.

Ongoing magic

To get seeds for next year, leave one or two beans to overmature before picking. Then let them dry out and split.

Herbal sun tea

All these herbs like to grow in full sun and prefer moist, well-drained soil mixed with a little grit.

Herbs have been grown all over the world for centuries for their flavor and goodness. Some herbs have been used to make healthy refreshing drinks, such as herbal teas. Using the warmth of the sun during the day, you too could make some delicious tea from the international herbs you've grown.

Which herbs?

Be careful to choose the right parts of each herb to make different sun teas. We used:

Jar 1: The flowers and leaves of bergamot, or bee balm.

Jar 2: The stems and leaves of epazote.

Jar 3: The leaves of mint and lemon verbena together.

Jar 4: The leaves of lemon balm and catnip together.

Jar 5: The leaves of borage.

Jar 6: The leaves of lemon grass cut into 2 in (5 cm) lengths.

Lemon verbena   Mint

Epazote   Bergamot

1 **Ask an adult** to drill holes in the base of an old suitcase. Place a trash bag inside and punch holes in it. Add a layer of grit and then fill the case with potting soil mixed with some grit.

2 **Imagine** the surface of your suitcase is a world map. Arrange the herb plants you have bought according to the position of the country where they originated.

Hold the plant by the root ball as you gently remove it from its pot.

3 **For each plant,** make a deep hole in the soil that is large enough to fit the root ball. Water the plant, then gently squeeze it out of its pot and place the plant into the hole.

4 **Fill in the soil** around the plant. The base of the stem should be level with the soil surface. Once you've planted all your herbs, water them around their roots.

Make flags to show where the herbs originated. For example, borage originally came from Syria and epazote from Mexico.

Make sun tea

Shake the jar every now and then throughout the day.

1 **In the morning,** pick 3 to 4 tablespoons of the fresh leaves, flowers, or stems, depending on the herb you want to use, and put them into a jar.

2 **Add 2–3 cups** (½ liter) of water. Put the lid of the jar on securely and shake the mixture thoroughly. Leave the jar in a place that gets full sunlight.

3 **In the late afternoon,** the tea should appear a rich green in color and be warm to drink. Strain the contents and serve. Throw away any unused tea.

Strawberry boot

Place your strawberries in full sun. The best soil is well-drained, rich in nutrients, and slightly acidic. The plants will produce fruit within 12 weeks.

Strawberries are trailing plants, which means that they trail down from containers—even containers like a pair of old rain boots! So buy some small strawberry plants, plant them in boots filled with potting soil, and wait until the strawberries start appearing. They'll be "boot-i-ful"!

You will need:

Rubber boots
Craft knife
Crushed eggshells
Vaseline
3 strawberry plants per boot

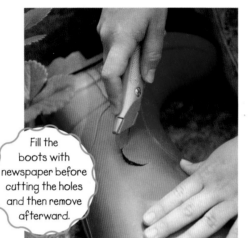

Fill the boots with newspaper before cutting the holes and then remove afterward.

1 **Ask an adult** to drill some holes in the sole of a boot. Use the craft knife to cut two holes the size of each plant's root ball into the sides of the boot.

2 **Fill the boot** with a little gravel for good drainage, making sure it also goes into the toes. Then fill with potting soil up to the first hole.

Place the boots near to your front or back door if it is a sunny spot, since birds are not likely to go there.

4 **Make a deep hole** in the top of the boot and add in a third strawberry plant. Use your fingers to press the soil gently around the plant, making sure the crown is level with the soil.

5 **Cover the surface** with eggshells as decorative mulch and to stop snails and slugs from getting to the leaves and fruit. Water the plants well around the roots for the first couple of days.

6 **Do not overwater** as the strawberry plants grow— they can rot. But do feed them with tomato fertilizer every one or two weeks until they begin to fruit.

Loosen the roots by brushing off the soil before inserting.

3 **Gently insert** a plant through the hole by holding the root ball. The top of the roots (the "crown") should be level with the soil surface. Continue to fill the boot with soil and put in the second plant.

7 **Rub a ring** of vaseline around the boot to keep out slugs and snails. You can also cover the boot with netting to stop greedy birds from getting the fruit first.

Red currant refreshments

Like glittering rubies, red currants ripen on the bush from midsummer. Add these juicy jewels to fruit salads, or squash them to make a refreshing drink like this cordial. If you can't wait for your own bush, gather these gems from a nearby pick-your-own farm.

To pick, remove the entire cluster by hand, or use scissors to cut off the sprigs.

You will need:

2 cups (225 g) red currants, stalks removed
½ cup (100 g) raspberries
1¼ cups (240 g) sugar
14 fl oz (400 ml) cold water

1 Ask an adult to make a syrup by heating 1½ cups (240 g) sugar and 14 fl oz (400 ml) of water slowly in a saucepan, stirring gently until the sugar has dissolved. Boil for 3 minutes, then cool.

2 Put the fruit into a bowl and mash it together well, using the back of a fork or a potato masher. Place a damp dish towel under the bowl so it doesn't slip.

4 Cut the end off a clean pair of panty hose (make sure they're an old pair) or cut a square of clean muslin and stretch this over the top of a tall pitcher. Secure with a rubber band.

5 Pour the fruit mixture through the cloth, which will act like a fine strainer and allow only juice to pass through and collect in the bowl underneath. Leave this for an hour or two.

6 Mix the rest of the cooled syrup with the cordial. Pour this into a clean bottle and store it in the refrigerator until you need it.

A bush of your own...

Buy a young bush and plant it in a large container or directly into the ground. Choose a sunny open spot with a little shade. After a year or two, if you look after your plant, red currants will grow in abundance year after year.

In **early spring**, add a mulch of well-rotted compost to keep in the moisture and stop the weeds. Feed with a high-potash fertilizer. In **summer**, before the fruit ripens, cover the bush with a net to keep hungry birds away.

In **fall**, once the plant is established, take cuttings to grow more bushes. Choose strong, straight stems with lots of buds, and trim into 4-6 in (10-15 cm) lengths. Push into soil in a small pot, leaving a bit above the surface. Keep them moist, and in the spring they should start to grow.

Plant your cuttings into their own pots in the following fall. After four years, every **winter**, prune out two or three of the oldest branches.

3 **Into your mashed** fruit, pour 4 fl oz (100 ml) of the sugary syrup that was prepared earlier. Stir this mixture gently, but thoroughly.

7 **When you're ready,** pour a little cordial into a pitcher according to taste, and add water, sparkling water, or soda water to make a refreshing treat.

The finish line

Even at the end of the growing season, a gardener can have some fun. Flowering plants produce seeds that can be collected and stored until the time for planting in the next year. What would you like to grow again?

Collecting seeds

At the end of their life, plants produce and release their seeds to grow in new places. What seeds look and feel like tell us about how the seeds get away from their parent plants. A number of different ways can be used to collect them.

Airborne

Seeds that are blown away by the wind are often tiny, or, if larger, have hairlike parachutes or wings to keep them up in the air.

Collect the tiny seeds by placing an envelope over a seed head and shaking the envelope so that the seeds will pop out.

Collect the larger seeds by tapping the seed heads gently onto a hard surface.

Put the seeds inside a strainer and gently shake to remove any dirt.

Storing seeds

Once the seeds are dried out, place them in a clearly labeled envelope. Remember to write the name of the seed and the date it was stored. Keep the envelopes inside a cool, airtight tub to prevent the seeds from turning moldy.

Type of seeds:
Dwarf sunflower

Date collected:
September 25, 2010

Sow in spring

Top tip

Why not share some seeds with friends?

Eaten

Seeds inside a soft fruit or vegetable are eaten by animals, then pass through the digestive system and end up in animal droppings, ready to grow.

To collect these seeds, cut open fruits or vegetables and let their seeds dry out before storing.

Or, let the fruit or vegetable dry out first and then split it open to remove the seeds.

Hangers on

Seeds with sticky or spiked sides attach themselves to animals that brush past. They eventually fall off and, with luck, start to grow.

These seeds need to be collected carefully, since they can be prickly to touch.

So collect them using tweezers and then place them directly into an envelope.

11

Glossary

Annual
A plant that completes its whole life cycle in a year.

Bolting
When a plant produces a long stem with flowers that turn to seeds. This can happen if the plant doesn't get enough water during dry weather.

Cactus
A spiny plant that can store water inside its stem.

Climber
A weak-stemmed plant that uses other plants or man-made structures for support as it grows.

Compost
A rich mixture of decayed plants that is added to the soil.

Deadheading
Cutting off the dead flowers to encourage the plant to produce new flowers.

Disease
A condition caused by fungi, bacteria, and viruses that affects a plant's health and growth.

Fertilizer
A mixture that encourages plants to grow.

Flower
The part of a plant where the male and female parts are found. Flowers with bright colorful petals attract nectar-feeding insects to visit and in doing so pass pollen from the male part of one flower to the female part of another. This is a process called pollination.

Fruit
The part of a plant that forms when a flower is pollinated. The fleshy part protects the seeds inside.

Germination
When seeds sprout and start to grow.

Green gardening
A way of gardening that is environmentally friendly, encouraging wildlife and using homemade compost rather than artificial chemicals.

Leaf
The part of a plant that makes the plant's food. This is a process called photosynthesis. A leaf takes in carbon dioxide from the air and uses sunlight to join this with water to make sugar-based food.

Microgreen
A seedling that is ready to eat within 7–14 days.

Moist
Slightly wet.

Mulch
A thick layer covering the surface of the soil that keeps in the moisture, prevents weeds from growing, and helps protect the roots from cold. Some add nutrients to the soil.

Perennial
A plant that has a life cycle that lasts three or more years.

Pests
Any bug or animal in the garden that harms plants.

Propagator
A covered container that stays warm and moist to encourage seeds or cuttings to germinate quickly.

Recycle
To use materials again.

Roots
The underground parts of a plant that take up minerals and water from the soil and support the plant. Enlarged roots, such as carrots, store food and water.

Salad leaves
A mixture of uncooked edible leaves, such as lettuce and spinach.

Seed
A part of a flowering plant that contains a baby plant and a store of food to get it started.

Self-irrigation
A way of keeping soil moist at all times, without watering.

Sprout
A seed that has just begun to germinate.

Transplant
To move a young plant that has outgrown its pot into a larger container.

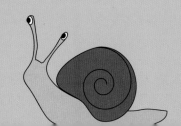

Index

alfalfa 48
alyssum 24
annuals 7, 22, 23
aphids 8, 39, 69
arugula 56
Asian greens 45, 60–61
avocado 34
beans
   azuki 49
   dwarf French 68–69
   lablab 35
   mung 48
bees 22, 23, 38, 39
beet 48, 56
birds 8, 18, 19
bolting 60
broccoli 56
butterflies 23, 38, 39
cacti 20, 21, 40–41
candytuft 8, 23
carrots 62–63
celery 57
chickpea 48
chocolate cosmos 34
cilantro 57
clarkia 22
clary sage 22
coleus 34
companion planting 9, 62–63
compost 8, 9, 13
containers 12–13, 34
   preparing 13
corn 35
corn salad (lamb's lettuce) 57
cornflower 23
cuttings 51
deadheading 7, 22, 25, 28
diary 5
fairy ring 21, 30–31
fenugreek 49
flowerpot people 21, 26–27
germination 6, 7, 20, 46
godetia 23
gourds 34
grasses
   cat grass 42
   Lucerne grass 42, 48
   ornamental 20, 30
   timothy meadow grass 43

green peas 48
hanging basket 36–37
herbal tea 35, 45, 71
herbs 22, 39, 44, 64–65,
   70–71
insects 8, 35
kebabs 44
kohl rabi 44, 45, 58–59
lacewings 8, 38
ladybugs 8, 38, 39
lanterns 30, 31
leaves 16, 34, 35, 36, 37, 56
leeks 62–63
lemon verbena 35, 70
lentils 49
love-in-a-mist 22
mallow 23
marigolds 8, 9, 21, 22, 24–25
microgreens 45, 56–57
morning glory 32
mulching 11
mustard and cress 48
nasturtiums 21, 22, 36–37
newspaper pots 13
pepper 64–65, 67
perennials 7
pest control 5, 6, 8, 45, 53, 55, 63,
   68, 69
pets 21, 42–43
pineapple 34
pizza garden 44, 64–65
poppies 20, 28–29
   Shirley poppy 22
propagator 6–7, 66
radishes 45, 52–53
rapini 56
recipes
   Asian stir-fry 61
   colorful kebabs 67
   cool kohl salad 59
   nasturtium salad 37
   pizza 65
   red currant cordial 74–75
   sprouting seed wrap 47
   sun tea 71
recycling 9, 12–13, 18–19
red cabbage 56
red currants 44, 74–75
repeat sowing 52, 54

salad leaves 54–55
seedlings 6, 44, 56–57
seedpods 22, 23, 29, 35, 38
seeds
   collecting 37, 76
   dispersal 76–76
   sprouting 6, 46–47, 48–49
   storing 77
self-irrigation system 10–11, 58
slugs 9, 24, 53, 55, 68, 72, 73
snails 9, 55,,72, 73
snow peas 46–47, 49
spinach 56
stepping-stones 16–17
strawberries 44, 72–73
sunflowers 8, 16, 20, 26–27
sunlight 4
sweet pea 33
swiss chard 57
tepee 20, 32–33
thinning 21, 45
tickle-me plant 34
tomato 64–65, 67
Venus flytrap 35
watercress 36, 45, 50–51
watering 6, 7, 11, 21, 51
windowbox 21, 38–39
worms 8
zucchini 16, 66–67